Artists in Profile

ABSTRACT EXPRESSIONISTS

Rachel Barnes

Heinemann
LIBRARY

What is Abstract Expressionism?

Abstract Expressionism was the name for an artistic movement that emerged in the USA during the 1950s. It was also known as the **New York School** since most of the important artists lived there, at least for a time. During World War II many influential artists had fled the fighting and persecution of Europe and ended up in New York. The Abstract Expressionist group were made up of artists who had either come from Europe or who were directly influenced by the styles and techniques of those who had.

Abstract Expressionism is a term used for art that uses elements of **Expressionism** in an **abstract** way. They were also influenced by **Surrealism**. Expressionist artists used symbols and particular styles of painting to express feelings or emotions. Surrealists tried to express the **subconscious** by using distorted but symbolic images. The Abstract Expressionists expressed things through the actual process of painting. The physical property of paint (what it was like) was what was important. The style and the subject (what the painting was of) had lost all significance.

The recognition of the Abstract Expressionists by the art world meant that for the first time the USA became known as an important force in **avant-garde** art. The term avant-garde is often used in art, and is used to describe anything radically new or different. The Abstract Expressionists fitted this description perfectly. For the first time it was the physical act of painting that was important rather than the end product.

Who were they?

The New York School was not, in the strictest sense, an artistic movement. The Abstract Expressionists included artists who had each developed their own individual styles. But there were enough similarities in the way they thought about and approached painting that gradually the group became known as the Abstract Expressionists.

Jackson Pollock, Willem de Kooning, Helen Frankenthaler, Lee Krasner and Franz Kline all became recognized for a technique called 'action painting'. This was where spontaneous physical movement and gestures were used to produce paintings. The term 'action painting' was originally used by the art critic Harold Rosenberg. He was referring to Jackson Pollock, who became famous for his 'drip' paintings. Pollock used a revolutionary new technique, which involved dripping, pouring or squirting the paint from syringes directly onto the canvases. We now use the term 'action painting' in a wider sense to refer to any technique of making a painting with energetic and spontaneous application of paint.

Other artists who also fall under the title of Abstract Expressionists include Mark Rothko, Barnett Newman and Clyfford Still. These artists invented a softer, calmer technique where paint is applied with brushes in large areas, or 'fields', of colour. There is often no frame or edge to the painting and the expanse of colour covers the whole picture surface. This technique became known as 'colour field' painting.

■ *Men Playing Basketball,* by Elaine de Kooning
Although the title of this work refers specifically to an action-packed event, the brushstrokes used by the artist communicate a feeling of dynamic movement rather than actually describing the players.

Both the 'action' and 'colour field' painters shared methods and ideals. Paint is applied in bold, simple brushstrokes, dribbles or splashes, with blocks of colour to make the maximum visual impact. The huge physical size of the paintings matched the artists' grand philosophical ideas.

Abstract Expressionists all shared a philosophy about painting. Paintings were a search for 'truth', or the hidden meaning of life. The artists tried to find a way of painting that did not have to follow any particular style or 'school' of art. This way people would not associate the painting with anything else. They would just look at it as a painting and form their own ideas of what it meant.

World War I

The daily lives of the American-born Abstract Expressionists would not have been greatly affected by World War I (1914–18). However, some of them were born in Europe and might have had first-hand experience of family, friends or relatives being called up to fight, and of the shortages of food and goods.

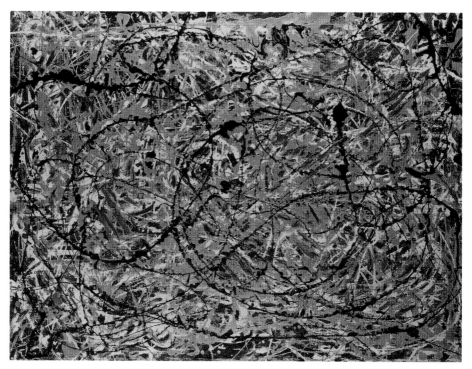

Undulating Paths, by Jackson Pollock (1947)
Made in the year Pollock invented the drip painting, this painting expresses the feeling of wildness and freedom and the overwhelming sense of the paint's texture, which the artist was able to achieve with his new method of working.

The Great Depression

The Wall Street Crash in New York is often seen as the starting point of the **Great Depression**. Wall Street is the stock exchange centre for the USA. In October 1929 the stock market 'crashed'. The value of companies, and the 'stock' that people had bought in those companies as an investment, suddenly became nearly worthless. People panicked and tried to sell off vast numbers of shares. This made the problem even worse. The USA's economy slumped, ending the financially well-off 'boom' years of the 1920s. Businesses collapsed and thousands were made penniless virtually overnight.

The Depression was felt all over the world, especially by countries relying on US loans. In 1929, the USA stopped lending money abroad and by 1930 nearly 2000 banks collapsed as people rushed to withdraw their savings. Three years later there were over 12 million people unemployed in the USA.

Federal Art Project

The US Government stepped in to help struggling artists as the Depression deepened. In 1934 they set up the Public Works of Art Project and started to book artists to work on **murals**. The Works Progress Administration (WPA) started up the Federal Art Project (FAP) in 1935. The FAP began to **commission** artists to do **easel painting** and sculpture as well as murals. Artists included in the group were paid around 23 dollars a week – just enough to survive. More than a 100 community art centres were opened across the USA, employing around 6000 artists – almost three-quarters of whom were living in New York. The FAP also formed a community of artists for the first time, mostly in Greenwich Village in New York. Artists such as Jackson Pollock, Willem de Kooning, Lee Krasner and Mark Rothko were all involved. In fact those who did not qualify because of their income, such as Barnett Newman who had a teaching job, felt like they were missing out. Newman said, 'I paid a severe price for not being on the Project with the other guys; in their eyes I wasn't a painter; I didn't have the label.'

World War II

World War II (1939–45) was fought across much of Europe and Asia and this time the fighting really was worldwide. Technology had advanced since World War I – aircraft and tanks were used far more. Ordinary people were even more affected. Advances in bombing technology meant their towns and cities were more likely to be bombed. People were evacuated to safer areas and families broken up, while shortages of food and clothing were commonplace.

New York during World War II was full of artists who had fled Europe. Key members of the **Surrealists**, such as Salvador Dalí and Max Ernst, and other great **abstract** and **Cubist** artists, such as Fernand Léger, Piet Mondrian and Marc Chagall spent the war years in New York. These artists were a source of inspiration for many Abstract Expressionists. Soon New York, rather than Paris, was established as the centre of art.

These European artists found life in New York very different from life in Paris. The cafés of Paris provided places for artists to meet and discuss their work. However, there was no such tradition in New York. Also many of the artists found themselves in different areas of New York because of the need to find housing quickly when they arrived. Art galleries like the Museum of Modern Art and the Julien Levy Gallery began to take the place of the cafés as artists' meeting places. However, it was the private gallery of Peggy Guggenheim that was the most important. Peggy Guggenheim came from a wealthy family who supported the arts and she was an important art dealer. She was also married to the Surrealist artist Max Ernst. Her New York gallery, The Art of This Century, was a key place for the Abstract Expressionists to exhibit in the 1950s.

Surrealism

The Surrealists, who had dominated the art scene in Paris before World War II, had a major impact on Abstract Expressionist painters. The Surrealists were fascinated with the workings of the **subconscious** mind and the writings of the pioneer **psychoanalyst**, Sigmund Freud. They painted distorted dreamlike images that represented the subconscious. Mark Rothko's early work was strongly dependent on Surrealist concepts and ideals, especially those of Joan Miró who used abstract signs and symbols to express basic themes of life.

Post-war USA

The New York School became a force to reckon with during the late 1940s partly because Europe was still caught up in the aftermath of World War II. A good deal of European artistic creativity was put on hold with so many artists called up to fight, but significant art was still being made, much of it in response to the events of the war and, in particular, the **Holocaust**. But it was not enough to prevent the art world shifting its centre to another, safer country.

The USA, of course, also played a significant role in the fight against Germany and the Nazis. The crucial difference was that the actual fighting did not take place on US soil. Consequently, whilst Europe suffered a period of economic depression, the USA was about to enter a time of relative wealth.

Reaction to world events

The Abstract Expressionist painters came to believe that their art must be abstract. It should not represent the corrupt material world that they had experienced. Abstract Expressionism was a response to a variety of factors that include earlier art movements and the political and social circumstances of the USA in the 1930s and 40s.

■■ *Untitled,* by Mark Rothko (1953)
The three-tiered effect of Rothko's colour fields has sometimes been seen as expressive of the concept of earth, heaven and hell. Using abstract colour with no frames Rothko wanted to express feelings through colour alone.

Helen Frankenthaler b. 1928

- Born in New York on 12 December 1928.
- Has lived mainly in New York.

Key works
Mountains and Sea, 1952
The Bay, 1963
The Other Side of the Moon, 1995

Helen Frankenthaler invented an original, highly expressive form of Abstract Expressionism. She used vivid, luminous colours and rejected paintbrushes in favour of her own technique of soaking the canvas with paint.

She was born on 12 December 1928 in New York City to Martha Lowenstein and Alfred Frankenthaler. She had two older sisters, Marjorie and Gloria. Her background was cultured and middle class; her father was a New York State Supreme Court Justice, although he died when Helen was only twelve.

She first attended Brearleys, an exclusive New York girls' school, before moving to the more liberal Dalton School. She left Dalton when she was seventeen but while there she was the favourite pupil of the celebrated Mexican **mural** artist Rufino Tamayo. She later said he liked her because she painted such good Tamayos. 'I used his medium literally; a third turpentine, a third linseed oil and a third varnish,' she recalls. Tamayo was the first professional artist she had ever met and from the start she was fascinated with his uncompromising approach to his work. She said later that he helped her realize what a serious and hardworking commitment it took to become an artist. He also taught her 'practical methods and materials; how to stretch a canvas with neat corners, how to apply the brush'.

While studying with Tamayo, she visited the old Guggenheim Museum on Seventy-second Street, which was near her family's apartment and Tamayo's gallery, Valentine. This was an important early exposure to advanced European art. As a teenager she often went to exhibitions at the Museum of Modern Art with her sister, Marjorie. On these outings she began to learn how to look at art, to analyse and understand the elements of each work. She retained a vivid memory of Salvador Dalí's *Persistence of Memory*, his famous **Surrealist** painting of a melted watch. 'For the first time I really looked and I was astonished,' she wrote of this experience.

As she was still only sixteen, Frankenthaler stayed on in New York for a semester after her high school graduation, continuing to study with Tamayo. In the spring of 1946, she left to attend Bennington College, where Paul Feeley had just become head of the art department. He was also to become a strong influence on her work. When she left three years later, she took off for Europe travelling to Amsterdam, London, Zurich, Brussels and Paris.

On her return to New York she met the painters Lee Krasner, Jackson Pollock and Elaine and Willem de Kooning. She also met the influential art critic Clement Greenberg. Gradually over the next few years she began to show her work at other venues, the Jewish Museum and the Whitney Museum of American Art. She also began teaching art on adult education programmes.

Frankenthaler was hugely inspired by Jackson Pollock's invention of drip painting and, as this photograph of her at work confirms, used similar methods herself.

For the following five years, she and Greenberg spent a great deal of time together. As a critic Greenberg wielded a huge influence over the direction of Abstract Expressionism. Together, the artist and the critic attended exhibitions, analysed paintings, went to galleries, museums and the regular Friday night meetings of the Artists' Club. Often, they took trips to the country to paint from nature. Frankenthaler used these trips to explore a **representational** style and method of painting. She did not keep much of this work. However, one piece that remains is an **Expressionist** portrait of Greenberg at his easel, painting a landscape.

In terms of Frankenthaler's future development, however, the great event of 1951 was Jackson Pollock's exhibition at the Betty Parsons Gallery. Pollock's 'drip' paintings, invented four years previously, changed the course of her art. From this time on Pollock became Frankenthaler's mentor (person who helps and advises another).

Greenberg took her to visit Pollock and his wife at their home in East Hampton the following spring. Here Frankenthaler saw Pollock's paintings rolled out or spread out on the floor and began to appreciate how he worked.

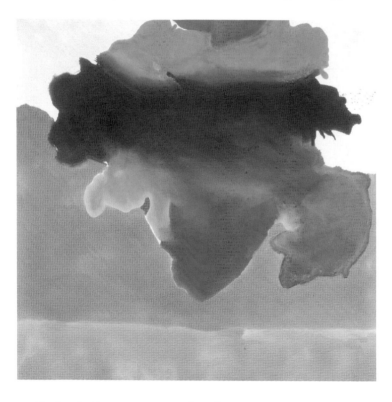

■ *The Bay,* by Helen Frankenthaler (1963)
Initially influenced by Mark Rothko's colour fields, Frankenthaler delighted in using bright colours to suggest the beauty and magic of the natural world.

She saw in his revolutionary technique a radically different approach to making paintings. He took the canvas off the easel and painted straight down from all sides. He abandoned the traditional brushes and oils in favour of enamel and a variety of dripping instruments. Frankenthaler was inspired by Pollock's ideas. She began to develop her own new ideas and employ them. From these explorations grew her style of 'action painting', working in a completely different way to traditional or representational art.

A few years later she would meet another hugely important artist, who would also change the course of her life, but in this case emotionally as well as professionally. In 1958 Frankenthaler married the painter Robert Motherwell. They travelled extensively throughout France and Spain for several months on their honeymoon, stopping to paint in a rented French villa in St Jean-de-Luz.

The marriage was not destined to last. (Motherwell had been married twice before and would marry again after his twelve year marriage to Frankenthaler.) But during the early years, they were very happy, both artists benefiting from the encouragement and support of each other.

Initially the marriage might have impeded Frankenthaler's wider recognition as an artist. Motherwell was one of the major voices of Abstract Expressionism. He was almost fifteen years older than her and had had more time to become established. Yet by her forties, Frankenthaler's own individual, poetic response to Abstract Expressionism was increasingly seen as a force in its own right. In 1969, a huge **retrospective** exhibition at the Whitney Museum confirmed this. Since the exhibition, which received huge acclaim from both critics and public, there have been many shows on both sides of the Atlantic.

Morris Louis 1912–62

Morris Louis (born Louis Bernstein) was born in 1912 in Baltimore. He first studied painting at the Maryland Institute of Art (1929–33) then worked under the WPA **easel painting** project (1937–40). Louis' work was initially influenced by the sharp lines and **geometric** forms of **Cubism**. Later he became influenced by Abstract Expressionism. This was particularly so after 1952, when he was introduced to Jackson Pollock's 'drip paintings'. He was further influenced by an important meeting with Helen Frankenthaler, who taught him to pour acrylic paint directly onto the canvas without using brushes. His work brought together the moods and scenes of the soft, evocative, painterly style of Monet and **Impressionism** with Abstract Expressionism. Like Monet, however, he was frequently dissatisfied with his work and went through periods of destroying much of it. He died in Washington in 1962.

Arshile Gorky 1905–48

- Born in Khorkom, Armenia on 15 April 1905.
- Died in Sherman, Connecticut, USA on 21 July 1948.

Key works
Some in Khorkam, 1936
Waterfall, 1943
One Year the Milkweed, 1944

Arshile Gorky was born Vosdaing Adoian on 15 April 1905, in Turkish Armenia. His father deserted the family in 1908, running away to the USA in order to avoid serving in the Turkish army. During World War I there were terrible massacres in Armenia and Gorky's family was forced to flee the country in 1915. Gorky's family was in desperate poverty, so bad that his mother died of starvation in March 1919. Following her death, Gorky and his sisters joined a refugee ship and crossed to the USA to rejoin their father.

■ *Gorky was well aware of his good looks and loved to dress in flamboyant clothes. But his extrovert nature concealed a darker side which sadly became more pronounced as he got older.*

Gorky did a number of jobs while also studying to be an artist at the Rhode Island School of Design at Providence Technical High School. When he was 21 he left for New York. Here he first of all studied, and then later taught, at the Grand Central School of Art. It was at this point that he decided to change his name, passing himself off in a newspaper as a cousin of the Russian writer Maxim Gorky. He seemed not to realize that Maxim Gorky's name was in actual fact also a pseudonym (invented name to replace real name).

From the start Gorky dressed the part of the artist, wearing flamboyant clothes that set off his handsome, romantic looks. He explored many different artistic avenues in his early years as a painter. Initially he favoured the works of the **Post-Impressionist** Cézanne before becoming, like fellow Abstract Expressionist Jackson Pollock and many other artists of this time, completely obsessed with the **Cubist**, Picasso. For a long time Gorky was not recognized as a serious artist, as people accused him of simply imitating other people's work.

For a while during the **Great Depression**, Gorky was too poor even to buy paints and canvas. But he was determined to continue with his art at all costs. In 1930, he was included in a show at the Museum of Modern Art, 'Forty-Six Painters and Sculptors under Thirty-Five'. In 1934, he had his first one-man show at the Mellon Gallery in Philadelphia. He married his first wife, Marny George in 1935, but the marriage did not last.

By the mid-1930s he had developed his own highly individual style. He moved away from the **geometric** style and began to use sweeping, natural shapes. A little later he made the acquaintance of André Breton, the leader of the **Surrealist** group of painters, who agreed to write the catalogue preface for Gorky's one-man show at the Julien Levy Gallery in New York. At the beginning of the 1940s Gorky married his second wife, Agnes Magruder.

Gorky was at last a success in the art world. However, his luck was not to last. On 26 January 1946 a fire raged through his studio in Sherman, Connecticut. It destroyed about 30 paintings. Then, late in February 1946, he had to have an

operation for cancer. On top of all this, in December 1947, his father died. Gorky became unstable and accused his wife Agnes and his friend Matta of having an affair. Agnes, worn out by his jealousy felt she had no option but to leave Gorky. Finally, on 26 June 1948 he was injured in a bad car crash, breaking his neck and paralysing his arm so that he was unable to paint.

It was the combination of all these misfortunes that caused Gorky, who had always been a temperamental, highly-strung man, to take his own life on 21 July 1948. It was just at the time that his art, for which he had struggled for so long, was becoming widely recognized.

■■ *Waterfall*, by Arshile Gorky (1943)
Gorky's style of painting, like his personality, was excitable. Waterfall *wonderfully evokes the sensation of cascading water.*

Franz Kline 1910–62

- Born on 23 May 1910 in Wilkes-Barre, Pennsylvania, USA.
- Died on 13 May 1962 in New York, USA.

Key works

Siskind, 1958
Black Iris, 1961

Kline was born in Wilkes-Barre, Pennslyvania on 23 May 1910. He was the second child of four. Neither of his parents were originally from America. His father came from Hamburg and his mother was English. When Kline was just seven years old, his father committed suicide. The emotional scars were to haunt him throughout his life. In 1919, two years after his father's suicide, the nine-year-old Kline was sent to an institution for fatherless children, Girard College in Philadelphia where he stayed for six years. Kline was unhappy here and was finally rescued by his mother in 1925.

Whilst Kline was at high school, he had an accident in football practice. It was during his recovery that he started to draw in earnest. Kline's career as an artist began with his decision to become an illustrator.

■ *This famous photograph of Kline was taken in the last decade of his life when he was at last beginning to receive recognition. He sits in his studio, surrounded by his dramatic black and white paintings.*

In 1931, he went to Boston University and afterwards to Boston Art Students' League. In 1935 he went to England. His mother was English and he had always been fascinated by all things English. He enrolled at the very conservative Heatherley's School of Fine Art in London.

Kline met a young dancer named Elizabeth Vincent Parsons at Heatherley's. She was a ballet dancer in the Sadler's Wells ballet and modelled at the art school. In 1938 Kline returned to New York where he would spend the rest of his life, and Elizabeth followed him. They got married and their marriage was initially happy.

However, Elizabeth suffered from a mental illness and her health was probably not helped by their poverty. They were so poor that they found it almost impossible to keep up with rent payments or afford to run a house. Three times they were evicted and there was never any stability to their home life. In 1948, Elizabeth's condition deteriorated and she had to go into Central Islip State Hospital where she would remain for the next twelve years.

During his first years as an artist Kline had worked in a **representational** style. He had favoured life-drawing and illustrations. However, the 1950s saw Kline painting and expressing himself in a new way. In 1950 Kline had his first one-man show at the Egan Gallery. Here he showed his new **abstract** style. His striking images, made up of bold, straight brush-strokes, were very well received. Influenced by Oriental calligraphy – the art of decorative writing – Kline had discovered his method almost by accident by projecting a small drawing onto the wall to create the effect of an enlarged microscopic detail. This style was to characterize the rest of his work.

In the last decade of his life before heart disease killed him at 51, Kline enjoyed a good deal of fame. He died on 13 May 1962.

■■ *Meryon,* by Franz Kline (1960-61)
This work is typical of Kline's love of using huge black brush strokes on a white background.

Elaine de Kooning 1918–89

- Born 12 March 1918, in Brooklyn, New York, USA.
- Died on 1 February 1989 in Long Island, USA.

Key works

Self-portrait, 1946
Baseball Players, 1953
Sunday Afternoon, 1957

Elaine Marie Fried was born on 12 March 1918 to Marie Catherine, an Irish Catholic, and Charles Frank, a German Protestant. Her intelligent, eccentric mother was a strong influence on Elaine, providing a good role model of an independent woman. Elaine grew up to be precocious, competitive and outgoing. When asked about her artistic talent, she said, 'I never made a decision about being a painter. When I was five, I made drawings like all children.'

Elaine regularly visited New York's Metropolitan Museum of Art to see the great European masters. As soon as she graduated from high school she entered Hunter College, but dropped out the following year because she wanted to become a painter. 'I just couldn't stand not having a paint brush in my hand,' she said. 'I didn't feel that I had time for college. I knew what I wanted to do. And while college was interesting, it wasn't that important to me then.'

She entered the Leonardo da Vinci School in New York City, where she later remembered: 'I drew all day every day'. Always conscious of her own beauty, she also worked as a model for other artists, to help pay her tuition fees.

Elaine was still a student when she first met the artist Willem de Kooning in 1936, although she had already heard a lot about him. She fell instantly in love. A mutual friend recalled: '[Willem] seemed interested in her in a way that he had never been interested in any of the other women around him. He ... was prepared to be monogamous ... he didn't want any other woman.'

The marriage, which took place in 1943 was to last – on and off – for almost fifty years, although they spent as long apart as they were together. It was an open marriage – from the start both had affairs with other people. They only separated in 1954 when Willem had his daughter, Lisa, by another woman. But before she left him, de Kooning had done everything in her power to help establish him, neglecting her own art in the process. The relationship was also destructive. By the time de Kooning left Willem, both had become alcoholics.

After they separated de Kooning was able to develop her own gifts as a painter. A lot of de Kooning's art focused on men and during the 1950s she painted sports stars, such as basketball players and bullfighters, to express her interest in movement.

De Kooning recovered from her drink problem and managed to support herself by working as a visiting professor at universities across the USA. She also became well known as an art critic. When she heard that Willem was ill in 1976 she went back to look after him. Under her guidance his career revived. Later on however, there would always be controversy as to whether his paintings might not have been at least partially done by de Kooning.

Although it was de Kooning who had returned to take care of her husband, it was her health that collapsed first. She died in 1989 from lung cancer, caused by heavy smoking.

■■ *Self-portrait*, by Elaine de Kooning (1946)
Elaine de Kooning was extremely conscious of her beauty and shows it to good advantage in this self-portrait.

Willem de Kooning 1904–97

- Born on 24 April 1904 in Rotterdam, Netherlands.
- Died of Alzheimer's on 19 March 1997, in Long Island, New York, USA.

Key works
Evacuation, 1910
The Visit, 1966
Woman in the Water, 1967

Willem de Kooning, along with Mark Rothko and Jackson Pollock, was one of the great Abstract Expressionists. Like them he was powerfully inventive, developing a radically new approach to painting. And like them he also had a darker, self-destructive side.

He was born on 24 April 1904 in Rotterdam in the Netherlands. When he was only three his parents, Cornelia Nobel and Leandert de Kooning, divorced. He was left in the care of his mother, who appears to have abused him, certainly mentally and possibly physically.

When he was twelve he was apprenticed to a local firm of commercial artists and decorators. He also went to night classes at the Rotterdam Academy of Fine Arts and Techniques and continued to study there until 1924. Many of the Dutch art students he met there idolized the work of the artist Piet Mondrian. Mondrian painted in an **abstract**, **cubist** style, with sharp black lines filled with bright blocks of colour. At the time de Kooning dismissed traditional painting as only 'good for men with beards', and said 'the idea of a palette was rather silly'. De Kooning and his fellow students were more interested in exploring new ideas.

But as he grew up, de Kooning became dissatisfied with life in Rotterdam, and began to long for adventure. In 1926, at the age of 22, he made one of the biggest decisions of his life. He stowed away on a ship and went to the USA. At the time, the reason he left was not to further his art. He wrote: 'I didn't expect there were any artists here. We never heard in Holland that there were artists in America. There was still the feeling that this was where an individual could get places and become well off, if he worked hard ... When you're about nineteen and twenty, you really want to go up in the world, and you don't mind giving up art.'

When de Kooning got to the USA he found work in New Jersey as a house painter. He was pleased with the money he could earn – nine dollars a day was quite a large salary. He stuck at this for about five months and then decided to look for work doing illustrating and applied artwork. He worked on a portfolio of examples of work. He was hired straight away, expecting to be earning a much higher wage for this skilled work than he was for house painting. It was a shock therefore when he received his wage packet at the end of the first two weeks. He said: '... the man gave me twenty-five dollars, and I was so astonished that I asked him if that was a day's pay. He said, "No, that's for the whole week." And I immediately quit and went back to house painting.'

So ended his first exploration of the art world. In 1927 he packed up and left New Jersey and ended up in New York. Again he found work in commercial art, painting signs, working on displays for shops and more painting and decorating jobs.

He did not completely abandon his art though. In New York de Kooning made an important friendship with an artist called Arshile Gorky. He shared a studio with him for some time. De Kooning was still working as a house painter and sign painter, which helped him develop painting techniques that he taught Gorky. But he also felt that he learned a lot from Gorky's intuitive approach to art: 'Gorky didn't have [training] ... And for some mysterious reason he knew more about painting and art – he just knew it by nature – though I was supposed to know and feel and understand, he really did it better.'

■■ De Kooning never lost his Dutch accent and was known in his younger days in New York as 'the handsome Dutchman'.

■■ *Woman VI*, by Willem de Kooning (1953)
*This energetic, dynamic image of a woman was part of a series exploring
movement and sexuality.*

During the **Great Depression**, de Kooning struggled to make ends meet. Like many fellow artists, he went to work on the Federal Art Project. Unfortunately, in 1936, the government banned immigrants from the project, especially those like de Kooning who had come to the USA illegally.

Yet despite the struggle, he was gradually becoming better known. In 1940, he was asked to design the sets and costumes for a production of the ballet *Les Nuages* for the Ballets Russes de Monte Carlo.

In 1936, de Kooning met Elaine Fried, whom he would later marry in 1943. Elaine was beautiful, energetic and a tremendous support to her husband. She did a great deal to promote his work and was partially responsible for his recognition as one the great Abstract Expressionists. Both of them had affairs throughout the marriage and seemed to accept this as normal. But it inevitably had a destructive effect. They separated in 1954 after de Kooning had a daughter, Lisa, by another woman. They both had a drink problem by this time. Although Elaine was eventually cured, she was unable to help de Kooning to beat his alcoholism.

In 1950 de Kooning changed his artistic style drastically. Most famous from this period perhaps is his *Woman I* painting. De Kooning had started to reject the abstract style of his previous black and white paintings. He adopted a more **Expressionist** style and the figure is recognizable as a woman. In 1951, de Kooning's painting, *Excavation*, won the Logan Medal and Purchase Prize. It was recognized as one of the most important pieces in the development of Abstract Expressionist art. A couple of years later six of his paintings of women were shown at the Sidney Janis Gallery in New York, causing a sensation.

Although his drinking and life style was becoming increasingly wild and uncontrolled, by 1960 de Kooning was becoming famous. In 1968 a huge **retrospective** exhibition was held at the Stedelijk Museum in Amsterdam. This was his first return to the Netherlands since he had left, penniless, aged 22.

De Kooning's last years, which he spent on Long Island, saw his alcoholism get steadily worse. He went downhill both physically and mentally. The early stages of Alzheimer's disease also contributed to his decline. He continued to paint, helped by Elaine who had returned in 1976, but there has always been a lot of dispute as to how much of this work he did himself. It has been suggested that Elaine or one of the painters employed in his studio worked on some of his canvases at this time, and that they were falsely passed off as de Kooning's own work. Elaine herself died in 1989 from lung cancer. De Kooning lived another decade, suffering increasingly from his illness. He died 19 March 1997 on Long Island.

Lee Krasner 1908–84

- Born on 28 October 1908 in New York, USA.
- Died 19 June 1984 in New York.

Key works
Little Images, 1943
Continuum, 1949
Solstice (series), 1949

Lee Krasner was born Lena Krassner in Brooklyn on 28 October 1908. Her family were Russian-Jewish immigrants who had only just arrived in the USA. Krasner went to school in Brooklyn, then transferred to the only local high school in New York that taught art to girls, Washington Irving High School in Manhattan. From 1926 to 1928 she studied at the Women's Art School of the Cooper Union. She also modelled and waitressed to earn money. She still hoped to become an artist and took part in the Federal Art Project (FAP).

Self-portrait, by Lee Krasner (1931–33)
Krasner was a highly independent artist in her own right, yet she had to fight to have this acknowledged after she married Pollock.

During her twenties Krasner discovered a skill for **political activism**. She took part in political demonstrations on behalf of the Artists Union and was jailed on a couple of occasions. Being part of the FAP meant she was considered an artist, but Krasner was not happy with her development and in 1937 she returned to her art studies, this time with the artist Hans Hofmann.

By 1941, Krasner was gaining a reputation as an up and coming artist, but was hoping for a break to help launch her career as a painter. It came in the form of an invitation to participate in an important art show for the design firm of McMillen Inc. Jackson Pollock's work was also being shown. He lived near by and Krasner decided to go and say hello. The relationship blossomed and by the following autumn, they were living together.

Recognizing that Pollock had great artistic gifts, Krasner made the decision to dedicate much of her energy to helping promote his work. During this time, Krasner continued to develop her own artistic style, often reworking her earlier paintings, such as *Milkweed*, with great success.

She helped Pollock stage his first one-man show at Peggy Guggenheim's The Art of This Century Gallery. She also helped him with his on-going battle with alcoholism. The couple moved out of New York City to the comparative tranquillity of nearby Long Island in 1945. They married shortly after and country life seemed to be working – from 1948, for a two-year period, Pollock stopped drinking.

Krasner's growing success as an artist came at a time when Pollock found it increasingly hard to paint. Their relationship was in ruins. Krasner reached a crisis point in both her personal and professional life when Pollock died in a car crash in 1956. Krasner continued to promote his work after his death. But her own art was now at last being recognized. In the early 1970s, she gave up looking after Pollock's work to concentrate on her own. The **feminist movement** took up her cause and she responded, demonstrating in protest about the Museum of Modern Art's neglect of female artists.

Her place as an important artist in the Abstract Expressionist movement was assured when she was included in the huge survey show, 'The New American Painting and Sculpture: the First Generation' staged at the Museum of Modern Art in 1969. In 1983 the Houston Museum of Fine Arts opened a full **retrospective** of her work, which travelled throughout the USA. Krasner died on 19 June 1984, before the show reached New York.

Untitled, by Lee Krasner (1949)
Krasner was a committed abstract painter from early on in her career. Her work often reveals a love of pattern for its own sake.

Robert Motherwell 1915–91

- Born on 4 January 1915 in Aberdeen, Washington, USA.
- Died on 16 July 1991 in Provincetown, Massachusetts, USA.

Key works

Pancho Villa, Dead and Alive, 1943
Elegy for the Spanish Republic (series), 1948-90
At Five in the Afternoon, 1949
Je t'aime (series), 1953-57

Robert Motherwell was a key member of the Abstract Expressionist group. Unlike most of the Abstract Expressionists, Motherwell had a very privileged upbringing. While others were struggling to make a living during the Depression, Motherwell was touring Europe. One of the most intellectual of the group, he was also a writer, studied theories and ideas about art and was a talented printmaker and draughtsman.

Robert Burns Motherwell was born on 4 January 1915 in Aberdeen, Washington. His parents were Scottish and Irish. His father worked as chairman of a bank. He wanted his son to go into law or business. When Motherwell was a teenager, the family moved to San Francisco. Motherwell attended the Otis Art Institute in Los Angeles, a San Francisco High School and then Moran Preparatory School, where he first looked at modern art in the *Encyclopaedia Britannica*.

Motherwell later went to Stanford University. Because at that time, there were few art collections in California, he still got very little opportunity to see art at first hand, which he very much wanted. But he would always remember one of his earliest experiences:

'One day ... a friend said he was going to a cocktail party and would I like to go ... he said, "I heard you were interested in pictures, and this will be a place with a lot of real painting"... It was Michael Stein's and I saw some Matisses and they went through me like an arrow. No one could have told me that Cézanne and Matisse were not the greatest and my mistake, my innocent mistake, was to suppose that modern art was all French.'

Motherwell graduated from Stanford with his philosophy degree in 1937. He then went to do a PhD at Harvard between 1937 and 1938. Following this he travelled around Europe with his father and sister.

■■ *Motherwell photographed in later years by which time he was enjoying huge fame and considerable wealth as one of the most important of the Abstract Expressionists.*

This was a hugely important experience; it was his first exposure to European literature, themes and artists, which would exert a huge influence on his art. The trip also gave Motherwell a great taste for travelling in Europe, something he would do whenever the opportunity arose in later life.

This trip was also his first encounter with the Irish novelist James Joyce whose work would affect him deeply. James Joyce was a modern author who wrote in a style called 'stream of consciousness'. He did not follow the rules of grammar or punctuation, instead he wrote as he thought; the words flowing unchanged from his mind onto the page. No conventions, punctuation or style was used to get in the way of the words, and therefore, the meaning. This technique was rather like what the Abstract Expressionists were trying to achieve with their art. Motherwell first came across Joyce's work when he bought a copy of his book, *Ulysses*. Motherwell recalled, '... My father took me to Europe and the first stop was Paris. The book stalls were still open, and I got this marvellous paperback of Joyce's *Ulysses*: I began to see what Modernism was.' He later painted a picture, which became famous, called *A Rose For James Joyce*.

Elegy to the Spanish Republic (Basque Elegy), by Robert Motherwell (1967)
Motherwell's brand of Abstract Expressionism often dealt with politics, such as this bold and powerful image, symbolic of a new phase in Spanish history.

In 1939, after this influential trip and to his father's dismay, Motherwell decided not to go back to Harvard but to become a painter. He moved to New York to study with an important artist and writer called Meyer Schapiro. Through him he met the **Surrealist** artists living in New York, notably Roberto Matta Echaurren, who became an important friend. He travelled with Matta to Mexico, where he spent four months painting, absorbing the colours of Mexican folk art. On the ship on the way, Motherwell had met a young Mexican actress, Maria Emilia Ferreira y Moyers who would soon become the first of Motherwell's four wives.

Under the influence of the Surrealists he took up 'automatism' or automatic writing and drawing. This was where each artist might write a word or draw a line, which did not necessarily have anything to do with the other words or lines. The end result was a poem or piece of art that had just come about 'by accident'. This idea was something the Abstract Expressionists spent a lot of time studying. In 1942 Motherwell was included in an exhibition in New York called 'First Papers of Surrealism'.

Back in New York, his career as an artist was quickly taking off. He had moved away from **figurative art** and began to paint in an abstract way, often just making a patchwork of brilliant colours, lines and marks. He abandoned the planning stages and started each painting with no set ideas. In 1944 he had his first one-man show at The Art of This Century Gallery, thanks to the owner Peggy Guggenheim. In 1945 he signed a contract with the dealer Samuel Kootz, which would last for the next ten years.

It was at this time Motherwell met other Abstract Expressionists including Barnett Newman and also Mark Rothko, who was to become a life-long friend. He fell into a pattern of teaching classes at the influential art college Black Mountain College in the summer, and then spending the winters on Long Island.

In 1948 Motherwell, along with other artists including Rothko, set up a school called 'Subjects of the Artist' in Greenwich Village, New York. He also did a lot of writing and editing at this time. He edited the Documents of Modern Art series, which was responsible for bringing the theories of European artists to the American public.

■ *Untitled D, by Robert Motherwell (1970)*
*In 1970 Motherwell declared: 'Most people ignorantly suppose that artists
are the decorators of our human existence ... But actually what an artist is,
is a person skilled in expressing human feeling... ' Abstract Expressionists
wanted to get away from the realism that had so far dominated US art.*

Motherwell's wife Maria complained that she felt isolated on Long Island, so in 1948 they moved back to New York City. But the marriage was by now failing and they divorced the following year. That same year Motherwell met his second wife Betty Little in Reno. She gave birth to two daughters Jeannie and Lise. It was also at this time that Motherwell began his friendship with David Smith, one of the most important American sculptors of the 20th century. Motherwell mourned him deeply when Smith was killed in a motor accident in 1965.

Motherwell organized much of his work into different series. The most important series was probably *Elegy to the Spanish Republic*, which included over a hundred paintings created during a forty-year period (1948–90). The paintings were linked to Motherwell's feelings about the Spanish Civil War and he suggested that the theme of the series was 'insistence that a terrible death happened that should not be forgot'.

The late 1950s saw a change of art dealer and another change of wife for Motherwell. Dealer Sidney Janis took him on in New York and the same year he met the painter Helen Frankenthaler. They married in 1958. This relationship was to last much longer and be far more fruitful than his earlier marriages; he and Helen had a great deal in common as abstract painters. They immediately went off to Europe for their honeymoon, staying to paint for several months in the South of France.

Motherwell returned to have his first major **retrospective** at Bennington College. He was now internationally acknowledged as one of the major forces of the **New York School**; honours were heaped upon him in the last two decades of his life. He had retrospectives in Sao Paolo (1961), Pasadena (1962), the Museum of Modern Art, New York (1965), Mexico City (1968) and Barcelona and Madrid (1980). In 1982 the Bavarian Museum of Modern Art opened a room devoted to Motherwell's art works.

Motherwell's marriage to Helen Frankenthaler ended in 1971, but in the year of his divorce he met the photographer Renate Ponsold, whom he married the following year. They remained happily married until Motherwell's death on 16 July 1991, at Cape Cod, Massachusettes, after a series of operations on his heart.

Barnett Newman 1905–70

- Born on 29 January 1905 in New York, USA.
- Died on 4 July 1970 in New York, USA.

Key works

Onement I, 1948
Stations of the Cross (series), 1958–1966
Who's Afraid of Red, Yellow and Blue?, 1967

Barnett Newman was associated with the Abstract Expressionists, although at first appearance his work seems very different. Instead of working in the way the other Abstract Expressionists did, with 'action' painting, Newman preferred to use the 'colour field' technique. In contrast to other artists, like Jackson Pollock or Franz Kline whose work developed on the canvas as they were painting, Newman carefully planned his ideas before even lifting a brush. His extraordinarily simple canvases have more in common with Mark Rothko's work. They are painted in large, soft, blocks of colour with sharp defining lines through or across them. His techniques pave the way for the next major New York movement – **Minimalism**.

Newman was born in Manhattan on 29 January 1905 into a Polish–Jewish family. He was the eldest of four children. His father, Abraham, had built up a successful clothing manufacturing company in the USA after arriving as a penniless immigrant. The family lived a good life in the suburbs of the Bronx, thanks to his father's successful business. Newman attended a local school and a Hebrew school. Unusually for an artist, in particular for the Abstract Expressionists, Barnett later remembered his childhood as idyllically happy.

He became fascinated by art as a teenager, playing truant from school to spend whole days in the Metropolitan Museum of Art. At seventeen, he persuaded his parents to let him enrol at the Art Students League while also finishing his last year at high school. He continued to study at the Art Students League while attending the City College in New York from 1923 to 1927.

Despite his attraction to art, there had always been pressure on Newman to work in his father's business. In the end a compromise was reached and he made a deal with his father. They agreed that he would work with his father for two years if at the end of it he could retire with $100,000 and pursue his own interests.

In contrast to his easy life before, the 1930s were a tough time for Newman. Disaster came with the Wall Street Crash in 1929. Although Abraham Newman refused to sell the business off, it was in desperate trouble. For the next ten years Newman struggled alongside his father to save the failing company. At the same time he brought in extra money by teaching high school art. Although this must have been deeply frustrating for someone with big ambitions to become a painter, he later denied feeling bitter about it. He claimed that many of his experiences had actually taught him valuable artistic principles. He had learned about: '... the meaning of form, the visual and tactile nature of things; how to take a rag and make it come to life. I learned the difference between a form and shape, for instance, I learned that women's clothes are painting and men's clothes are sculpture ... Soft sculpture...'

■ *Newman had to wait much longer than his fellow Abstract Expressionists to achieve the recognition he deserved for his unique contribution to the movement.*

In 1934 Newman met a young teacher called Annalee Greenhouse. Their first meeting was not promising: Newman loved to argue and debate and the two of them ended up having a row about the merits of the composers Mozart and Wagner ending with Annalee storming out! They married in 1936 and Annalee was a staunch support through the difficult years, of which there were many.

Not long after his marriage, Newman reached a point of complete despair about his art, suffering a kind of artist's block. 'Painting is finished, we should all give it up,' he told his artist friend Adolf Gottlieb and he did not paint for five years. During this time he threw himself enthusiastically into studying botany (plants), geology (rocks) and ornithology (birds).

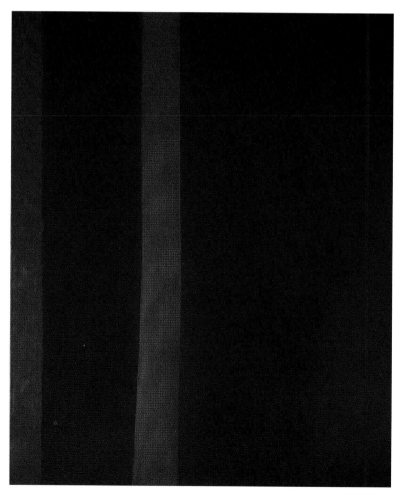

■■ *Adam*, by Newman Barnett (1951-52)
This is a famous example of Newman's 'zip' paintings, where a strong vertical line breaks into the colour. It took Newman many years to find his own way of responding to Abstract Expressionism.

For many artists such a sustained period of inactivity might spell the end, but not for Newman. After almost a decade of not working he destroyed much of his previous work and started afresh. In 1944 he worked on a series of drawings based around seeds and patterns of growth. Soon after this he rented a studio close to Willem de Kooning. His important break as an artist came with his painting, *Onement I* in 1948.

With *Onement I* and the paintings that followed, he developed an innovative way of working. He would mask off areas of his canvas with tape. By painting over the tape and then removing it Newman was able to get perfectly straight and sharp lines, which he referred to as 'zips'. His works from this period all contain the 'zips'. Over time he played with different edges, colours, numbers and widths, but the zip was there in one form or another.

Meanwhile Newman was also active as an art critic and curator (person in charge of putting on an art exhibition), helping to promote the reputation of fellow Abstract Expressionists – or the new American art, as it was called. He also organized two exhibitions of **primitive art** for the Betty Parsons Gallery.

His loyal support of the group made it particularly painful for Newman when his first one-man show at Betty Parsons Gallery in 1950 was severely criticized by his fellow artists. His show consisted of paintings like or inspired by *Onement I*, with its orange stripe or 'zip' painted on a red-brown background. The controlled simplicity of Newman's paintings appeared at odds with the expressive emotionalism of work from the other Abstract Expressionists. Newman, however, always claimed that there was an emotional, or spiritual content in his art.

Newman's financial problems continued after the disaster of his first two one-man shows and he again toyed with the idea of giving up painting and returning to the fashion trade. He did however have one important supporter. The influential critic Clement Greenberg felt that a show that had caused so many artists to react so violently, even if they didn't like the work, must have some value.

It was not until the late 1950s that Newman's paintings began to make the breakthrough he had so long dreamed of. In 1958, four of his paintings were included in New York's Museum of Modern Art's show, 'The New American Painting'. His now rapidly spreading reputation was secured with the exhibition 'Stations of the Cross' at the Solomon R. Guggenheim Museum in 1966.

Newman died of a heart attack on 4 July 1970 in New York.

Jackson Pollock 1912–56

- Born on 28 January 1912 in Cody, Wyoming, USA.
- Died on 11 August 1956 in a car crash in East Hampton, New York, USA.

Key works

Naked man with a knife, 1938
Summertime, 1948
Lavender Mist: Number I, 1950
Blue Poles II, 1952
Yellow Islands, 1952

Jackson Pollock was arguably the most important pioneer of Abstract Expressionism and one of the most revolutionary painters of the 20th century. He abandoned the tradition of **easel painting**, executing his works on the floor.

Paul Jackson Pollock was born on 28 January 1912 at Watkus Ranch, Cody, Wyoming. His mother, Stella May McClure, and father, Le Roy Pollock, both of Scottish-Irish descent, were born and raised in Tingley, Iowa. Jackson was their youngest son and he had four elder brothers, Charles Cecil, Marvin Jay, Frank Leslie and Sanford Le Roy.

Whilst Pollock was still a baby the family moved to California, then a little later to Arizona. For the next few years there would be constant moves between the two states as his father struggled to make ends meet. When Pollock was nine, Le Roy Pollock took off altogether leaving his wife Stella to struggle with her unruly boys. She was not good on discipline and early on her youngest was developing a wild side to his character and was often in trouble at school. When Pollock was four years old he had an accident when he cut off the top of his index finger whilst playing at chopping wood.

In 1922, Pollock's brother Charles had enrolled at Otis Art Institute in Los Angeles and was regularly sending home copies of the art magazine *The Dial*, which was Pollock's first exposure to modern art.

In 1926, Pollock graduated from Grant Elementary School in Riverside, and enrolled at Riverside High School where he joined the Reserve Officers' Training Corps (ROTC). Although Pollock was only fifteen, he was drinking heavily and was expelled from the ROTC because he punched a fellow student while drunk. He left Riverside High School the following spring and in the summer of 1928 the family moved to Los Angeles.

■ *The photographer Hans Namuth took a series of now famous films and photographs of Pollock in action, dripping and squirting the paint onto his canvas laid down on the floor of his studio.*

Pollock enrolled at the Manual Training School where he concentrated on art, but in March 1929 he was expelled for disciplinary problems. In September 1929 he was allowed back into the Manual Training School, but was soon expelled again. These were difficult painful, years for Pollock who as yet had found no positive direction. Trying to deal with his feelings of insecurity and unhappiness by drinking was the start of a pattern that tragically would dog his whole life.

As a child growing up in the West, Pollock discovered Native American culture. As he grew older he became fascinated by Native American art and their religious custom of making ritual sand paintings on the floor. At the Manual Training School he was introduced to the teachings of the mystical poet Krishnamurti. 'Fall in love with yourself and you fall in love with the truth' was one of Krishnamurti's sayings that strongly affected the rebellious Pollock in his early years.

At the age of eighteen, Pollock went to join his brother Charles in New York with the intention of becoming an artist. At the New York Art Students League he was taught by Thomas Hart Benton. Pollock was strongly influenced by his work. Benton had tried to come up with a 'uniquely American' way of painting, and the subject matter for his paintings was often drawn from the country's early frontier history. The young Pollock was also attracted by Benton's hard drinking, tough-man image – perhaps not the best role-model for a young man who already had alcohol problems of his own.

Over the next ten years, Pollock would live on the brink of extreme poverty as he took a series of jobs as a lumberjack and a cleaner to sustain his life as an artist. In 1938 the strain became intolerable; he suffered a major nervous breakdown that took six months to recover from. With his brother Sanford's encouragement he began psychiatric treatment for alcoholism under a Jungian analyst. Jung was a **psychoanalyst** who used the workings of the **subconscious** mind to analyse and treat his patients. The ideas greatly influenced Pollock's approach to his paintings. Many of them seem to reflect a search for some deep, spiritual, unconscious meaning behind life.

In 1941 he met the artist Lee Krasner. They would not marry for another four years, but Lee was to become an invaluable support. Pollock's big breakthrough came in 1942 when he met the influential art dealer Peggy Guggenheim. She started to show his work in her gallery, The Art of This Century. In 1944 Pollock showed some work in an intellectual magazine called *The Nation*. His talent was spotted by the influential art critic Clement Greenberg, who hailed Pollock as author of 'some of the strongest paintings I have yet seen by an American'.

From this time on, he began to receive more recognition, although by no means all of it favourable. He continued to be desperately short of money.

Pollock invented his 'drip' paintings around 1947, soon after he and Lee had moved to Long Island. Working on the floor, he developed a way of painting in which he poured, dripped or splashed the paint onto the canvas, allowing gravity to play a part in how the work turned out. Walking around the painting, at times standing on it, Pollock became immersed in the act of painting. He became obsessed with the idea of leaving a record of himself in his work and incorporated handprints, footprints, urine and cigarette ash into his paintings. In a statement he made in 1947, Pollock described how he made his paintings: 'My painting does not come from the easel ... On the floor I am more at ease. I feel nearer, more a part of the painting, since this way I can walk around it, walk from the four sides and literally be in the painting.'

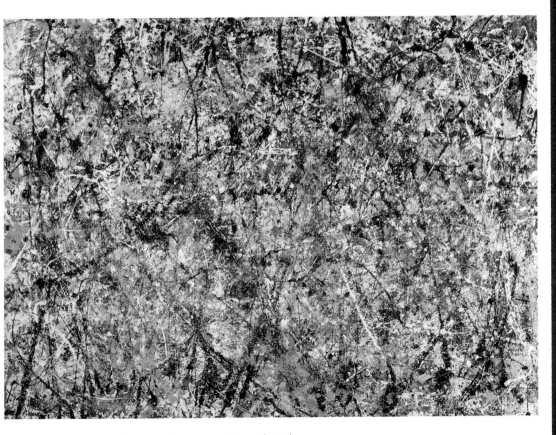

■ *Lavender Mist: Number 1*, by Jackson Pollock (1950)
This painting is one of the most celebrated of the drip style. The paint, in unusually gentle pastel shades, is densely layered to evoke wonderful sensations of a wild and profuse nature.

Pollock's new style was formed by a combination of many earlier experiences. These included the energetic **mural** painting of the Mexicans and the Native American sand paintings. Ritual dance also interested him. He was deeply interested in Jung, and in expressing the unconscious mind and was also a great admirer of **Cubism** and artists like Picasso and Miró.

In the last four years of his life, Pollock became increasingly depressed and dependent on alcohol. This was the point at which his wife Lee Krasner's own career was taking off. He reworked existing paintings, yet clearly he was suffering from artist's block, perhaps brought on by alcohol abuse. He had invented drip painting and revolutionized 20th century art, but having done so he seemed unable to develop.

By the spring of 1956, Pollock had not painted for eighteen months. He felt uncomfortable with how critics were interpreting his work. He struggled with the idea that Abstract Expressionist art was not supposed to have a particular subject. Pollock was always aiming to achieve this, to get as far from **figurative** painting as possible, but now felt he had failed to do so.

In a controversial interview with art historian Selden Rodman, he declared that art always, to a greater or lesser degree, had some sort of subject. If one painted from the unconscious then it was impossible to avoid recognizable figures emerging.

Blue Poles II, by Jackson Pollock (1952)
Pollock first became famous in 1949 when an issue of Life *magazine asked, 'Is he the greatest living painter in the United States?' Twenty years after he created* Blue Poles, *one of his most famous paintings, it was bought for $2 million by the Australian government.*

On 11 August 1956, Pollock was killed in a car crash, driving whilst drunk, late at night, with his mistress, Ruth Kligman, who survived the accident. He and Lee had temporarily separated. The Museum of Modern Art's exhibition, intended as a mid-career show, appeared instead as a memorial **retrospective**.

Hans Hofmann (1880–1966)

Hans Hofmann was born in Bavaria in 1880. As a young man he trained as an engineer, but in the late 1890s he enrolled in an art school where he discovered **Post-Impressionism**. From 1904 until 1914 he spent most of his time in Paris where he met Matisse, Picasso, Braque and Delaunay, from whom he received his basic training in using colour. He opened his own art school in Munich in 1915.

Hofmann concentrated on teaching from 1915 to 1938, so did very little painting himself. In 1940 Lee Krasner studied with Hofmann and she introduced him to Jackson Pollock and the other artists in this circle. Hofmann worked in a more formal way, painting from nature and using a subject for his work. He did not approve of Pollock's approach, his wish to express the unconscious through the act of painting and the paint itself.

It was not until the 1940s that Hofmann took off as an artist in his own right. His first one-man show was held in 1944, when he was 64, at Peggy Guggenheim's The Art of This Century Gallery. He died in New York on 17 February 1966.

Ad Reinhardt 1913–67

- Born on 25 December 1913 in Buffalo, USA.
- Died on 30 August 1967 in New York, USA.

Key works

Abstract Painting, 1959
Black Painting (Series), 1963
Abstract Painting, 1960-66

Ad Reinhardt was an artist who belonged to the end of Abstract Expressionism and the beginnings of **Minimalism**. He was deeply critical of many of the artists in New York. He said they prostituted their art for money whilst making ridiculous claims about it. He held the firm belief that 'art is art' and 'everything else is everything else' and the two should not be confused. He meant that artists who claimed that their work had some deep significance and power for life or death (like some of the Abstract Expressionists did) were frauds and were only worthy of contempt. Yet even though he was highly critical of them, his artistic style owed a lot to the Abstract Expressionists.

Ad Reinhardt was born Adolph Dietrich Friedrich Reinhardt in New York on Christmas Eve 1913. His parents were both immigrants, his father Russian and his mother German. Reinhardt's interest in art was even noticeable as a small child. He showed a flair for painting and won a competition aged seven. Later he won a prize for a pencil portrait of the boxer Jack Dempsey.

At the age of 22 he went to Columbia University and was taught by the famous art historian Meyer Schapiro. Reinhardt was interested in politics and writing as well as painting in his student days and he became the editor of the campus magazine *Jester*. He did not become serious about art until his mid-twenties, when he quickly got involved with **avant-garde** artists in New York. He left Columbia and managed to get a place on a public art project funded by the Federal Projects Administration (FPA). He discovered that the only form of art he was really attracted to was **abstract** art. 'I was born for it and it was born for me,' he said. Through the FPA he met other artists and in 1937 joined the American Abstract Artists group, whose aim was to promote abstract art in the USA. Many of the prominent abstract artists of the day were involved.

■■ *Reinhardt in a late photograph of him with one of his Black Paintings.*

The Federal Projects Administration supported Reinhardt until he got a job working as a journalist on the *PM* newspaper in 1941. The USA joined the war in 1942 after the bombing of Pearl Harbor by the Japanese. Reinhardt was drafted to serve as a sailor in the navy and was forced to leave the newspaper. The military '... didn't know what to do with me, so they made a sort of photographer out of me ... I was always thrown in with a bunch of kids. I was 29 then. I was called Pop. I was the old man of every outfit.'

■ *Abstract Painting No. 5*, by Ad Reinhardt (1962)
Reinhardt described these black canvases as 'the first paintings that cannot be misunderstood'.

He was discharged from the US Navy in 1945 and returned to *PM*. Not long after this he was fired, but he was given a teaching post at Brooklyn College. He taught for the rest of his career, but he never really rated himself as a very good teacher. Just before he died he said, 'I've been teaching for twenty years. I've never been called a good teacher. Incidentally, I'm proud of that.' During this time he was increasingly vocal about his opinions of the art world. He made **satirical** sketches and was generally critical, but still harboured dreams of becoming an artist himself.

His breakthrough came in 1946 with his first one-man show at the Betty Parsons Gallery. Over the next decade people began to invest in his work. He began to achieve commercial success. This was something that he had never sought for himself, and had always disliked intensely in others. To him it seemed unworthy and degrading to sell or 'prostitute' talent for money.

In 1953, he began to produce the canvases that he is best known for. He painted canvases in red, black and blue, patterned by barely visible squares in different tones and shades of the same colour. Seven years later in the 1960s all his paintings became black, square, uniform canvases. They were all painted on five-foot canvases and he described them as 'the first paintings that cannot be misunderstood'. Reinhardt was making the transition from Abstract Expressionism to Minimalism. In his minimalist paintings everything was reduced to a minimum, including colour, shade, shape or feature.

By the end of his life Reinhardt was making enough money from his art to fulfil another of his dreams and go travelling in the Far East. In 1958 he visited Japan, India, Persia and Egypt. Then, in 1961, he went to Turkey, Syria and Jordan.

In 1967 the Jewish Museum in New York held a huge **retrospective** exhibition of his work. Reinhardt had been an important member of the Modern Movement, and was proud to be seen as such. He had been a part of both the Abstract Expressionist movement and **Minimalism**. He claimed, half jokingly, that he was, 'the only painter who's been a member of every **avant-garde** movement in the last thirty years'. Reinhardt died on 30 August 1967 in New York.

Mark Rothko 1903–70

- Born on 25 September 1903 in Dvinsk, Lithuania.
- Died 25 February 1970 in New York.

Key works
Untitled (Yellow, Red, Orange), 1954
Light Red Over Black, 1957
Black on Maroon x 8 (The Seagram Murals), 1959

Marcus Rothkowitz was born into a Jewish family in the Lithuanian town of Dvinsk on 25 September 1903. Marcus had two elder brothers and one elder sister. Their father, Jakob Rothkowitz, was a pharmacist. The children's upbringing was very strict and traditional. They also grew up in a time when Jews were being persecuted and attacked in Russia. Rothko remembered the fear and the threatening environment for the rest of his life.

When Rothko was seven, his father **emigrated** to the USA with his two eldest sons. Three years later the rest of the family followed them to Portland, Oregon. Sadly, only seven months after the rest of the family arrived in the USA, Rothko's father died, leaving the family very poor. Rothko later said he felt permanently hungry as a child.

■ *Taken towards the end of his life, this photograph suggests the darker side of Rothko's nature, which despite huge fame and fortune would eventually overwhelm him.*

Unlike many artists, Rothko did not dream of becoming an artist in childhood or adolescence. Rothko was very able at school and won a scholarship to go to Yale University in 1921. However the scholarship was withdrawn after six months. This might have been as a result of prejudice against Jewish people. Rothko worked as a waiter and then as a delivery boy to pay for his education. At Yale he intended to be an engineer, but at the age of 20, after only two years at university, he decided to drop out for a bit to 'wander around, bum around, starve a bit'.

He headed for New York and a year later he had enrolled to study art at the Art Students League. In spite of two years of studying art here he would still always describe himself as a self-taught artist. A few years later he took a teaching job at Central Academy, Brooklyn, a Jewish school attached to the synagogue (place where Jewish people worship), to help support his initially very precarious life as a painter. He also worked part-time as an actor, took painting jobs backstage in the theatres and worked as an illustrator to supplement his income.

In 1932 Rothko married Edith Sacher, a jewellery designer. He also worked with many other Abstract Expressionists on the Federal Art Project. He got to know many people this way, and in 1935 met the Russian painter Arshile Gorky and another member of the **New York School**, Adolph Gottlieb. With Gottlieb he formed a group called 'The Ten' – a group of **Expressionists**, including Edith, who exhibited together over the next decade. In 1938, Rothko officially became a citizen of the USA. A couple of years after this he changed his name to the more American sounding Mark Rothko, although he only did this legally in 1959.

■■ *Central Green,* by Mark Rothko (1949)
Made the year that Rothko invented his colour fields, the colours at this stage in his career were usually clear and luminous.

During the war Rothko's first marriage failed and by 1944, when he met his second wife, Mary Alice (Mell) Beistle, his career as a painter was at last beginning to take off. By this time he had met other painters with similar ideas to his own, such as Jackson Pollock and Willem de Kooning.

Rothko's first one-man show was at the famous art dealer Peggy Guggenheim's The Art of This Century Gallery in 1945. This was the breakthrough he had long dreamed of, although it was not for another ten years that his paintings began to command huge sums.

Number 7, by Mark Rothko (1951)
In his works of this time, Rothko often paints his canvases in three tiers, sometimes interpreted as earth, heaven and hell. It was Rothko himself who said that his paintings were about 'tragedy, ecstasy and doom'.

Adolph Gottlieb (1903–74)

Adolph Gottlieb was born in New York on 14 March 1903. He left high school in 1919 and joined the Art Students League where he became friends with other members of the **New York School**. In 1935 Gottlieb and Rothko helped to establish an artists' group called 'The Ten', which was devoted to **Expressionist** and **abstract** painting.

In 1970, Gottlieb suffered a stroke which paralysed the left side of his body. However, he continued to paint from his wheelchair. Gottlieb died on 4 March 1974 in New York City.

By 1949, Rothko had moved on from his rather **figurative** expressionism to a kind of painting which he called his Colour Fields. He tried to express mood and emotion simply through the size and character of these colour fields. He did not want the subject matter of conventional, figurative paintings to get in the way and distract from the meaning of the painting. He saw the paintings as personal expressions of emotions and almost religious or spiritual feelings. He thought that he could make viewers have the same kind of spiritual experience just by looking at his paintings: '... the fact that lots of people break down and cry when confronted with my pictures shows that I communicate with those basic [human] emotions. The people who weep before my pictures are having the same religious experience I had when I painted them.'

Rothko was always unusually aware of how the viewer saw his work. He was preoccupied with the idea that each painting relied on the viewer for its meaning or value. If the viewer was sensitive and took time to look at the painting properly then it would 'live'. If a viewer was unsympathetic or not sensitive then the painting would just appear to be meaningless and 'dead'. It was 'therefore a risky and unfeeling act to send it out into the world'. He meant that he worried about his pictures almost as if they were alive. In 1952, he refused to submit two of his works to the purchasing committee of the Whitney Museum because of this 'deep sense of responsibility for the life my pictures will lead out in the world'.

Rothko's first full-scale **retrospective** at the Museum of Modern Art in New York was followed by a one-man show at the Whitechapel in London. But achieving huge fame on both sides of the Atlantic did little to dispel the depressive, anxious side to his nature that had always been there, but was made worse in later years by alcoholism. He became tremendously difficult, offending and permanently falling out with painter friends Jackson Pollock and Barnett Newman, after he claimed he had 'taught Barney how to paint'. His marriage to Mell also finally broke under the strain and he spent the last wretched months of his life alone, living and working in his studio, before committing suicide on 25 February 1970.

Clyfford Still 1904–80

- Born on 30 November 1904, in Grandin, North Dakota, USA.
- Died 23 June 1980, in Baltimore, Maryland, USA.

Key works
1963 A, 1963
July 1945, 1945
Untitled, 1961

Clyfford Still had grand ideas about his art. For him his own brand of Abstract Expressionism was a life and death matter, which would in time bring him both critics and fans. Although his aims and style had much in common with other Abstract Expressionists, Still remained independent and was always seen as a bit of an outsider. Critics continue to question whether he should really be categorized as an Abstract Expressionist.

Clyfford Still was born on 30 November 1904, in Grandin, North Dakota. His father, who was an accountant, moved the family to Spokane, Washington the following year. When Still was six years old, the family began to spend more time in Alberta after the Canadian Government opened the area to people who wanted to settle there. He loved his childhood in Canada and throughout his adult life would make frequent visits back there.

Still attended Edison Grammar School in Washington where he became especially interested in both art and music. After he had graduated he took frequent trips to New York to the Metropolitan Museum of Art to see the original versions of paintings that he had 'learned to love through the study of their reproductions', as he later wrote. His enthusiasm for art led him to enrol at the Art Students League in New York, but he very quickly left, finding the teaching unimaginative and unhelpful.

In 1926, he went to Spokane University in Washington. However, he soon decided to drop out and go back to his family in Canada. In 1931, despite dropping out of his course, he was awarded a teaching fellowship in art at Spokane University and found that he liked teaching. For the next ten years he would earn his living teaching at Spokane and then, after 1933, at Washington State College, Pullman. Although he got on well with the students he often found the staff unadventurous and unexciting, and their 'tried-and-trusted' approach irritated him.

Still's hopes to become a painter had not been dulled. Two summer fellowships at Yaddo artists' community in New York state, gave him the opportunity to re-evaluate what he wanted to achieve. At this time his style was mostly **figurative** and he worked on his style and technique by beginning to paint a series of **Expressionist** figure studies. Still's first exhibition came when he had just turned 30. Out of the 1500 paintings submitted to them, the National Academy of Design in New York chose to show one of Still's paintings in an annual exhibition. Despite this early recognition and success, and although he continued to paint whenever he could, Still left for California to work for a shipbuilding firm. Still's style and painting methods now grew into large **abstract** canvases using thick paint. These had much in common with the way Abstract Expressionism was developing in New York. The one-man show he was given at the San Francisco Museum in March 1943 was a breakthrough for him.

■ *Still sits third from the right in the back row, surrounded by fellow Abstract Expressionists including de Kooning, Newman and Pollock.*

Soon afterwards, Still met Mark Rothko for the first time whilst they were both teaching at a summer school at Berkeley in California. This was to be an important relationship for both men, although from the beginning it was competitive. Rothko helped Still, introducing him to Peggy Guggenheim who invited him to exhibit some paintings in the Autumn Salon at her The Art Of This Century Gallery. Later in 1946, she gave him a one-man show. He was nervous about the response his paintings would get and made plans to leave New York to avoid the opening.

Still did in fact return to Canada in 1947 to take up teaching again and build himself a small house, virtually single-handedly. He did not cut himself off from New York completely and kept in contact with Rothko who arranged to have some of Still's work shown. In spite of their friendship there were some tensions and rivalry between Rothko and Still. Rothko was always anxious to know what Still was up to, particularly to know how big his canvases were. Aware of this, Still mischievously sent back the message, 'Tell him I'm now doing paintings the size of postage stamps!' – which was of course very far from the truth. Still was anxious to protect his own work, about which he had some hugely grand ideas. He thought that by looking at his work people could find their way to a mental and spiritual freedom.

By the late 1940s, Still was well established in California and his paintings were commanding increasingly high prices. But he still harboured dreams of establishing an artist-directed school with Rothko in New York. Still was impatient and not willing to make compromises. Eventually he got fed up with his colleagues and their inability to make decisions. The school did eventually open but without Still's involvement as he grew frustrated by the length of time it was taking and went back to California.

Still's strong independence had probably helped him steer clear of the self-destructive tendencies, such as alcoholism and depression, shared by other members of the Abstract Expressionist group. But it also had its down side. He became increasingly difficult and reluctant to show his paintings. He even turned down the opportunity to show his work in Europe. He did, however, agree to stage a one-man show at the Albright-Knox Art Gallery in Buffalo, New York, in 1959, which proved to be a huge triumph. Throughout the 1960s he exhibited with the Marlborough-Gerson Gallery and he became increasingly well known. Unlike many other abstract expressionists, he lived long enough to see his name honoured as one of the great American painters of the 20th century. He died on 23 June 1980 in Baltimore.

Jamais, by Clyfford Still (1944)
Still always remained a little aloof from fellow Abstract Expressionists. This early powerful, dynamic and totally abstract image shows how instrumental he was in forging a new style in the early days of the movement.

The Next Generation

The influence of Abstract Expressionism was not limited to New York. It also had an impact on a group of artists working in California, particularly those working with the teacher David Park at the California School of Fine Arts in San Francisco.

Richard Diebenkorn 1922–93

Richard Diebenkorn was born in 1922 in Oregon, USA. As a child he was always drawing. He was influenced by many of the Abstract Expressionists. In 1940 he went to New York where he first saw the work of Robert Motherwell, amongst others, and during the mid-1940s he studied with Still and Rothko. In the early 1950s he became fascinated by Arshile Gorky's work. Diebenkorn died in 1993.

Minimalism

The **Minimalists** reacted against the ideas of the Abstract Expressionists. For example, the Minimalists believed that a work of art should be completely planned. They did not believe it should grow organically (develop as it was being painted) in the way that a Pollock 'drip' painting would. Key artists involved in this movement included Carl Andre, Dan Flavin, Don Judd, Robert Morris and Frank Stella.

Ellsworth Kelly b. 1923

Ellsworth Kelly was born in New York on 31 May 1923. He studied at the School of the Museum of Fine Arts in Boston from 1946 to 1947 before going to the École des Beaux-Art where many famous artists also studied. In France, Kelly discovered **Surrealism** and in 1950 met the Surrealist artist Jean Arp.

In 1954 Kelly returned to New York to work. He had a solo show in Paris in 1951, but his first one-man exhibition in New York did not take place until 1956. Three years later his work was shown along with that of Frank Stella in the exhibition 'Sixteen Americans'.

Frank Stella b. 1936

Frank Stella was born in 1936 in Malden, Massachusetts, USA. He studied painting at Phillips Academy in Andover before graduating from Princeton with a history degree. He was inspired by the work of Ad Reinhardt. Between 1959 and 1961, Stella painted simple, monochromatic paintings that were typical of Minimalism. Stella used ordinary black house paint to paint his canvases. Four of these works were shown in an exhibition called 'Sixteen Americans' in the Museum of Modern Art in New York, along with the work of Ellsworth Kelly, Jasper Johns and Robert Rauschenberg. Stella lives in New York and continues to paint.

■■ *Hyena Stomp*, by Frank Stella (1962)
*This painting was made with ordinary household paint. It is rigidly **geometric**, very unlike the expressive canvases of the Abstract Expressionists. Yet it is clear that the Minimalist painters, like Stella, were influenced by the movement as well as reacting against it.*

55

Timeline

1903 Mark Rothko born 25 September

1904 Willem de Kooning born 24 April; Clyfford Still born 30 November

1905 Barnett Newman born 29 January; Arshile Gorky born 15 April

1908 Lee Krasner born 28 October

1910 Franz Kline born 23 May

1912 Jackson Pollock born 28 January

1913 Ad Reinhardt born 24 December

1914 World War I begins

1915 Robert Motherwell born 4 January

1918 World War I ends; Elaine de Kooning born 12 March

1928 Helen Frankenthaler born 12 December

1929 Wall Street Crash

1934 US Government set up Public Works of Art Project

1935 US Government set up Federal Art Project

1936 International Surrealist exhibition in London

1939 World War II begins

1943 Willem de Kooning and Elaine Fried marry

1945 World War II ends; Jackson Pollock and Lee Krasner marry

1947 Jackson Pollock invents drip painting

1949 Mark Rothko invents colour field

1958 'The New American Painting' show at the Museum of Modern Art in New York; Robert Motherwell and Helen Frankenthaler marry

Glossary

abstract art removed from the recognizable. In terms of an art work it is not recognizable as an object, landscape, or person. A work where colour and shape are more important than what they represent.

avant-garde pioneers or innovators in any sphere of the arts

commission piece of work specifically requested by a group or art collector

Cubism early 20th-century school of painting and sculpture in which objects are shown as abstract geometric forms without realistic detail; often involving transparent cubes and cones

easel painting making a painting with the canvas on a wooden structure (easel)

emigrate to leave one's own country to go and live in another

Expressionism art in which traditional ideas are abandoned in favour of a style which exaggerates feelings or expressions

feminist movement movement that emerged in the 1960s to fight for equal rights for women

figurative art art in which recognizable figures or objects are portrayed

geometric from geometry, which is the study in mathematics of the angles and shapes formed by the relationship of lines, surfaces and solids in space

Great Depression time of economic depression which began in the US in 1929 when the stock markets crashed. Millions of dollars were lost in the value of shares sparking world wide depression which lasted several years.

Holocaust name given by Jewish historians to Hitler's 'final solution' during World War II when six million Jewish people were killed by the Nazis.

Impressionism movement started in France in the 1860s by Claude Monet and Pierre Renoir. it was a revolutionary and hugely influential movement; paintings were made on the spot in a matter of a few hours, as opposed to the months which academic painters spent and brush strokes were broken up with a new emphasis on the texture of the paint.

minimalism style of art developed in New York in the 1960s using a minimum of line and colour

mural painting made directly onto the wall

New York School another term for the Abstract Expressionist movement

political activism taking part in political activities

Post-Impressionism term which includes artists such as van Gogh, Cézanne and Gauguin – artists who developed the ideas of Impressionism further

primitive art simple naïve art made by an artist with no training

psychoanalyst person trained to treat patients suffering from anxieties and nervous disorders. It was developed by Sigmund Freud

representational art art depicting recognizable things in the real world

retrospective exhibition of an artist's work from beginning to end

satirical a playful mockery of foolish or evil practice

subconscious hidden level of the mind and the thoughts that go on there

Surrealism movement originally developed in Paris in 1921 that aimed to express the subconscious mind by the use of bizarre, irrational, absurd and dreamlike images

Resources

List of famous works

Helen Frankenthaler (b. 1928)
Mountains and Sea, 1952, private collection, on loan to National Gallery of Art, Washington DC, USA
Before the Caves, 1958, National Museum of Women in the Arts, Washington D. C., USA
The Other Side of the Moon, 1995

Arshile Gorky (1905–48)
Some in Khorkam, 1936, private collection
Waterfall, 1943, Tate Modern, London
One Year the Milkweed, 1944, National Gallery of Art, Washington D.C.

Franz Kline (1910–62)
Painting No.7, 1952, Guggenheim Museum, New York
Siskind, 1958, Detroit Institute of Arts
Black Iris, 1961, Museum of Contemporary Art, Los Angeles

Elaine de Kooning (1918–89)
Self-portrait, 1946, National Portrait Gallery, Washington D.C., USA
Baseball Players, 1953
Sunday Afternoon, 1957
Jardin de Luxembourg VII, 1977, National Museum of Women in the Arts, Washington D. C., USA

Willem de Kooning (1904–97)
Evacuation, 1910, Museum of Modern Art, New York
The Visit, 1966, Tate Modern, London
Woman in the Water, 1967, private collection

Lee Krasner (1908–84)
Continuum, 1949
Solstice (series), 1949
Primeval Resurgence, 1961, Museum of Contemporary Art, Los Angeles
Right Bird Left, 1965, Ball State University Museum of Art, Indiana, USA

Robert Motherwell (1915–91)
Pancho Villa, Dead and Alive, 1943, Museum of Modern Art, New York
Elegy for the Spanish Republic, 1948-90, Museum Ludwig, Cologne
Je t'aime, 1953-57, Staatsgalerie Moderner Kunst, Munich

Barnett Newman (1905–70)
Onement 1, 1948, Tate Modern, London
Stations of the Cross (series), 1958–66
Who's Afraid of Red, Yellow and Blue? 1967, Stedelijk Museum, Amsterdam

Jackson Pollock (1912–56)
Naked man with a knife, 1938, Tate Modern, London
Summertime, 1948, Tate Modern, London
Yellow Islands, 1952, Tate Modern, London

Ad Reinhardt (1913–67)
Abstract painting, 1959, Marlborough International Fine Art
Abstract painting, 1960-67, Guggenheim Museum, New York
Black Painting (Series), 1963, Tate Modern, London

Mark Rothko (1903–70)
Untitled (Yellow, Red, Orange), 1954, Kate Rothko's Collection
Light Red Over Black, 1957, Tate Modern, London
Black on Maroon x 8 (The Seagram Murals), 1959, Tate Modern, London

Clyfford Still (1904–80)
July 1945, 1945, Albright-Knox Art Gallery, Buffalo, USA
Untitled, 1961, National Gallery of Art, Washington D.C., USA
1963 A, 1963, Albright-Knox Art Gallery, Buffalo, USA

Where to see Abstract Expressionist artists
UK
The Tate Modern, London www.tate.org.uk/modern
These have some pieces of Abstract Expressionist art. The Tate Modern has a
room full of Rothko's murals and many of Jackson Pollock's works.

USA
The Museum of Modern Art, New York www.moma.org
Work by many of the Abstract Expressionists artists, including Kline, de
Kooning, Motherwell and Newman, is permanently on display.

Whitney Museum of American Art, New York www.whitney.org
Contains a wealth of works by contemporary American artists.

Guggenheim Museum, New York www.guggenheim.org
Works by many Abstract Expressionists including Kline, Motherwell, Pollock,
Reinhardt and Still.

National Gallery of Art, Washington DC www.nga.gov
Work by Abstract Expressionists such as Frankenthaler, Gorky and Still is
exhibited here.

Albright-Knox Art Gallery, Buffalo www.albrightknox.org
Much of Clyfford Still's work is held here.

Australia
Art Gallery of New South Wales, Sydney www.agnsw.com.aus
Works by Horn, Kelly and Stella exhibited.

Germany
Museum Ludwig, Cologne
Holds some of Motherwell's work.

Staatsgalerie Moderner Kunst, Munich
Holds some of Motherwell's work.

Internet Disclaimer
All the Internet addresses (URLs) given in this book were valid at the time of going to press.
However, due to the dynamic nature of the Internet, some addresses may have changed, or sites
may have ceased to exist since publication. While the author and publishers regret any
inconvenience this may cause readers, no responsibility for any such changes can be accepted by
either the author or the publishers.

Further reading

Most libraries and bookshops will have a selection of books on Abstract
Expressionist art, as well as biographies of some of the most famous artists.
Most of the books and biographies are written for adults, but there are many
reproductions of the artists' works which will be interesting for younger readers
to look at.

General
The Thames and Hudson Dictionary of Art and Artists is an excellent general
resource. It gives brief definitions of art terms and short biographies of many
artists from different backgrounds and schools.

Abstract Expressionism: The Critical Developments, Ed. Michael Auping, Thames and Hudson, 1987

American Abstract Expressionism, Ed. David Thistlewood, Liverpool University Press and Tate Gallery Liverpool, 1993

Art Since 1940: Strategies of Being, Jonathan Fineberg, Laurence King Publishing, 2000

Lives of the Great 20th Century Artists, Edward Lucie-Smith, Thames and Hudson, 1999

The 20th Century Art Book, Susannah Lawson, Phaidon Press, 1996

20th Century Art: 1940–1960 Art in Emotion, Jackie Gaff, Heinemann Library, 2000

The artists

Frankenthaler: Works on Paper 1949-1984, Karen Wilkin, Helen Frankenthaler, International Exhibitions Foundation, George Braziller Inc, 1985

Black Angel: A Life of Arshile Gorky, Nouritza Matossian, Chatto and Windus, 1998

Franz Kline, Harry F. Gaugh, Abbeville Press, 1994

Spirit of Abstract Expressionism, Elaine de Kooning, George Braziller, 1994

The Essential Willem de Kooning, Catherine Morris, Harry N. Abrams Inc., 1999

Lee Krasner, Robert Hobbs, Abbeville Press, 1993

Robert Motherwell on Paper : Drawings, Prints, Collages, Robert Motherwell, Arthur C. Danto, Stephen Addiss, Mary Ann Caws, Harry N. Abrams Inc., 1997

Barnett Newman, Ann Temkin (Editor), Tate Gallery Publishing, 2002

Jackson Pollock (Exhibition Catalogue), Tate Gallery Publishing, 1998

Jackson Pollock. A Biography, Deborah Solomon, Simon and Schuster, 1987

The Fate of a Gesture: Jackson Pollock and Postwar American Art, Carter Ratcliff, Straus and Giroux, 1996

About Rothko, Dore Ashton, 1983, Oxford University Press

Mark Rothko, 1987, Tate Gallery Publications

The Legacy of Mark Rothko, Lee Seldes, 1978, Secker and Warburg

Index